Caring For Your Body

WATER

Written by
Rebecca Phillips-Bartlett

KidHaven
PUBLISHING

Published in 2025 by
KidHaven Publishing, an Imprint of
Greenhaven Publishing, LLC
2544 Clinton St., Buffalo, NY 14224

Written by: Rebecca Phillips-Bartlett
Edited by: E.C. Andrews
Designed by: Ker Ker Lee

Cataloging-in-Publication Data

Names: Phillips-Bartlett, Rebecca, 1999-.
Title: Water / Rebecca Phillips-Bartlett.
Description: Buffalo, NY : KidHaven Publishing, 2025. | Series: Caring for your body | Includes glossary and index.
Identifiers: ISBN 9781534548985 (pbk.) | ISBN 9781534548992 (library bound) | ISBN 9781534549005 (ebook)
Subjects: LCSH: Water in the body--Juvenile literature. | Drinking water--Juvenile literature. | Self-care, Health--Juvenile literature.
Classification: LCC QP535.H1 P45 2025 | DDC 612'.01522--dc23

Manufactured in the United States of America

CPSIA compliance information: Batch #CW25KH
For further information contact Greenhaven Publishing LLC at 1-844-317-7404.

Please visit our website, www.greenhavenpublishing.com.
For a free color catalog of all our high-quality books, call toll free 1-844-317-7404 or fax 1-844-317-7405.

Photo Credits – Images are courtesy of Shutterstock.com.
With thanks to Getty Images, Thinkstock Photo and iStockphoto.

Recurring images – TeddyandMia, Pensiri. Cover – Tatevosian Yana, Linor R - pattern, Pensiri- icons. 4–5 – Khosro, BearFotos. 6–7 – fizkes, robert_s. 8–9 – Vikkella, PeopleImages.com - Yuri A. 10–11 – Elena Nichizhenova, ChiccoDodiFC. 12–13 – Prostock-studio, Nikola Solev. 14–15 – OlgaKhorkova, TinnaPong. 16–17 – Alter-ego, Hanna Rusina. 18–19 – Maximumm, avtk. 20–21 – MNStudio, Ground Picture. 22–23 – Kaganovich Lena, George Rudy, JOKE_PHATRAPONG.

CONTENTS

Words that look like this can be found in the glossary on page 24.

CARING FOR YOU

Your body is just one part of who you are as a person. However, your body is also your home. Caring for your body is an important part of caring for yourself.

Taking time to take care of yourself is called self-care.

Have you noticed that when you don't feel well, you also feel upset or sleepy? The way your body feels has a big impact on your mind. A healthy body can lead to a healthy mind.

A healthy body gives you more <u>energy</u> to do things you enjoy.

ALL ABOUT WATER

Water is one of the most important things on Earth. All living things, including plants, animals, and people, need water to live. In fact, more than <u>half</u> of your body is made of water.

People can only live for three or four days without water. Thankfully, almost three-quarters of our planet is covered by water. However, not all of this water is safe to drink.

WHY DO I NEED WATER?

Drinking plenty of water helps to keep you healthy. Water has many jobs in the body. The water in your blood helps to carry oxygen around your body. It also helps fight infections.

When you are sick, you need to drink more water than usual.

Your body loses lots of water throughout the day when you sweat, go to the bathroom, and even when you breathe. It is important that you replace this lost water by drinking.

Having enough water in your body is called being hydrated.

WHAT HAPPENS WHEN I DRINK?

After a few big sips of water, your brain realizes that you are drinking. The water moves through your body to get used by the organs that need it.

Water goes to the stomach, heart, and other important organs. Most of the water you drink is used by the blood. The leftover water goes to the bladder and comes out as urine, or pee.

Always remember to wash your hands after going to the bathroom.

HOW MUCH WATER DO I NEED?

Different people need different amounts of water to stay hydrated. The amount you need to drink changes as you grow up. It can also change based on the weather or what activities you are doing.

You will need to drink more water when it is hot and when you are exercising. If you are drinking the right amount of water, you will not feel thirsty.

It is best to drink small amounts of water often rather than one big drink.

I'M THIRSTY!

Feeling thirsty often starts with a dry mouth. Thirst is your body's way of telling you that you have not drunk enough. When you start to feel thirsty, have a drink of water.

Water will hydrate you quicker than any other drink.

Not drinking enough water can lead to dehydration. If you are dehydrated, you might start to feel tired or dizzy. Your pee will be a darker color than usual.

I DON'T LIKE WATER!

Now you know why you need to drink water, but what if you just do not like it? There are a few ways to help you stay hydrated even if you do not like water.

You could try:

- Adding fruit to your water
- Drinking water with ice cubes
- Keeping a water bottle with you
- Eating fruits and vegetables with lots of water in them, such as cucumbers, watermelons, and tomatoes

Only add fruit to water sometimes. Too much fruity water can harm your teeth.

WHY DO I SWEAT?

Sweat is your body's way of keeping cool. Sweat is mostly made of water and a bit of salt and sugar. It comes out of your body through tiny openings in the skin called pores.

Once the sweat is on your skin, it evaporates. This means it is pulled into the air and turned into a gas. As the sweat evaporates, your skin cools down.

Sweating uses water. Make sure you drink enough to replace the lost water.

A HEALTHY LIFESTYLE

Your lifestyle is the way you live your life. It is made up of all the things you do each day, including what you eat, how much you sleep, and the activities you do.

Drinking plenty of water is one part of a healthy lifestyle. All parts of a healthy lifestyle work together. Being well hydrated will give you energy to exercise. Exercising regularly can help you sleep well.

THANKING YOUR BODY

Your body does so much for you. Try to notice one great thing your body lets you do. Say a big THANK YOU to your body for letting you do this.

Noticing what your body does helps you understand how important caring for your body is.

Caring for your body is another good way to thank your body. Your body will probably thank you back by keeping you healthy and giving you lots of energy to do things you enjoy.

How will you care for your body today?

GLOSSARY

energy the power that makes living things able to move and live

gas a thing that is like air, which spreads out to fill any space available

half one of two equal parts of one whole

infections illnesses caused by dirt, germs, and bacteria getting into the body

organs parts of a living thing that have specific, important jobs to do

oxygen a natural gas that all living things need to survive

quarters four equal parts of one whole

INDEX